IDENTITY THEFT

Are You The Next Victim?
How to Prevent, Detect and
Recover from Identity Theft

ROBERT RODRIGUEZ

ANGELICO BOOKS

Table of Contents

Introduction:
Bullet-Proof Yourself
Against Identity Theft

I'm sure you're probably familiar with "traditional" identity theft, where someone steals your personal identifying information or credit card and uses it to make purchases. This is the number one form if identity theft with financial losses of close to $50 billion per year! It can destroy your credit, take months to unwind, and cost you thousands of dollars!

But did you know that the other forms of identity theft can be equally damaging?

The identity theft resource center divides identity theft into five different categories:

Criminal identity theft. An identity thief can commit crimes pretending to be you! This can mean that you might get pulled over for a routine traffic violation and get hauled into jail as a murderer or bank robber. Then you have to try to convince the courts that you are innocent, that you are the victim of the crime of identity theft.

Identity cloning. An identity thief can use your identity to go to school, work illegally, to get married, to basically become you in every day life. You might not find out until you get rejected for credit. This can be one of the most expensive forms of identity theft as the thief has created an entire life in your name.

Medical identity theft. An identity thief can use your identity (and insurance benefits) to get medical care, not only racking up huge bills, but getting their medical profile integrated into yours, so your doctor may be making health decisions for you based on the thief's information!

Child identity theft. An identity thief can use your child's social security number to get credit cards, drivers licenses, even buy a house. Often the child doesn't discover that they've had their identity stolen for years!

Concerned? You might well be as identity theft is on the rise, and most people are unaware, or overwhelmed about what to do about it.

Many people I've talked to don't understand identity theft. They might look at a little information on it and quickly feel overwhelmed. We just don't want to consider that they might experience identity theft.

Some people have read some, and do get their annual free credit report, but don't know the simple little tips and tricks they can use to stop an identity thief in their tracks.

I was one of them. I tried to get a credit card to expand my credit and was turned down because I already had too much credit. I looked into it and found out that I was the victim of financial identity theft. The thief stole my credit information, wreaked havoc by buying all sorts of things online, destroyed my credit, then stopped. All in less than six months!

It took me a lot longer than that to sort it all out, and in the process I learned a lot about identity theft and the simple ways you can avoid it. I tried to educate my friends about it, and they were firmly in the "it won't happen to me" camp until I got them to check their credit reports. 5 of them were victims of identity theft, one of them of medical identity theft which has cost her thousands of dollars and months of her life to sort out.

So I put together this book to share with others what I have learned.

47 Things an Identity Thief Doesn't Want You to Know

During my studies of identity theft I spoke to several people who were ex-thieves. Here are the 47 mistakes common people (like me) make that identity thieves really, really love.

1. I love it when you leave your mailbox unlocked. That provides me with an opportunity to glean all sorts of information about you from both your incoming and outgoing mail.

Checklist:

- **Letters** containing your personal information
- Bank notices
- Pre-approved credit cards or loans
- Billing statements
- Checks
- Merchant notices
- ATM card replacements
- Medical information
- Driver's license information
- Children's identifying information

There are a ton of things I can get from your unlocked mailbox. Maybe you think your neighbors will notice? Unlikely. I'm just 'a friend' you asked to pick up your mail. So thank you very much for making it easy for me.

2. You should be very alarmed when your mail is not arriving as scheduled. Thank you for being so complacent and calm about it. Giving the benefit of the doubt that your merchant, your bank, or even your loved ones forgot to send you your mail giving me the opportunity to get away with using the information longer. When your mail is not arriving on time that may mean that someone (like me) has gotten hold of it first.

3. Don't put a password on your smart phone. It's a hassle. It also makes it easy for me to get access to a lot of information about you easily when I steal your phone.

4. I can intercept your checks. Seriously, I can intercept the checks you send to anyone through mail. Mailing a check is not really the most secure way to pay someone—so keep on doing it for my benefit!

5. When you're buying things online, use your regular card rather than get a single use number from your credit card company. It makes it so that there is more of a chance I'll be able to swipe it when I hack the online store.

6. The dumpster is my favorite informa- tion mine. Like anyone's mailbox, the dumpster is simply a place for me to dig up information sources from different individuals. What do I normally find in the dumpster?

For starters, thrown out mail that contains personal information, financial statements, bank accounts and loan applications, old telephone bills, old credit card bills, old hospital bills, old insurance bills, damaged credit or debit cards, love letters (*you have no idea what gold I can find in your romantic correspondence*), college applications, and even a Social Security ID!

What do I call this very enriching endeavor? I call it <u>Dumpster Diving</u>.

7. I'm not afraid of digging through the Dumpster in broad daylight. Why shouldn't I? What's the worst thing that you can ask me while I'm getting dirty with the dumpster in broad daylight?

I can always give you, "*I accidentally threw out my husband's wedding ring after our fight*" or "*I dropped my wallet*" as excuses. Pretty lame? It works beautifully.

8. Skipping the shredder? That's brilliant. Just throw away your documents as is and make life easier for me. I don't even have to piece together those pieces of paper from your credit card company.

9. Don't bother with your free annual credit reports. You're probably safe and you have so many other things to think about! It gives me more time to use your identity.

10. Give me your health insurance card as a form of ID, or lend it to me if I ask to see it. That way I can get your number without having to sort through your trash. 30% of medical identity theft is by someone you know. Treat your health insurance card like a credit card and protect it!

11. Are you the forgetful type who lists down your PIN, social security number, or bank account numbers on a paper, notebook, or tissue? Thanks. You are spoon-feeding me.

12. A minor's social security number will surely come in handy for me. If I steal a minor's identity by using his/her social security number and posing as him/her, I can get away with it for years until that minor grows up and notices problems with his/her records. So the next time you have a document that contains your kid's social security number, date of birth or identifying information, make sure you throw it in the trash intact — don't worry, I'll only use it for a decade or so!

13. Credit card is good but debit card is better. There are a thousand hackers out there who make breaching retail databases a daily activity. I can always buy your information from them. On top of that, I can have direct access to your bank accounts through your debit card. With your credit card I can only go up to your credit limit, and they'll probably call you for an unusual purchase. With your debit card I get direct access to your accounts and can drain them dry. Remember — cash is king. There's not as much damage I can do by stealing your cash.

14. Leave your purse available at a yoga or exercise class so I can easily access your ID & credit cards take photos of them and put it back so you don't report it.

15. If it's not your practice to be vigilant about your bills or account balances, that's good for me. Sometimes you get all-too caught up with the things that you do—family, career, and studies—so you don't have time to check your bills and account balances. Thank you for that. I use your credit, debit card or ATM card all the time, so by not checking your balances, you're giving me freedom and security. And for an identity thief, there isn't such a thing as too much freedom and security.

16. If you get an email from your bank asking you to click on a link and go to a form to fill in information, do it. It will take you to a web site I've set up to look like your bank where you can enter all your personal information, and I can get it!

17. I'm the "friendly" guy tailing you when you use your ATM. It's not like I'm stalking you or something. I'm just spying on your PIN codes, your usual gestures, your account balances…

I can always observe and replicate the things that you do when you are facing the ATM. The next time you find out that your ATM card is lost? I'm probably using it.

18. Noticed something strange sticking in your ATM card slot? I can install a skimmer in the card slot of most ATM's. That device can capture your card information, and most importantly, your PIN. The next time you see an ATM that looks strange, go ahead and use it!

19. Contactless credit card reader's are new technologies that make it easier for me. Did you know that I can scan the chip in your credit card using a mobile hand held device? So, if you think using a smart card so you don't have to swipe is a good idea, I suggest you reconsider your thoughts and do some research. Here's a nice article I found on the subject for you. http://www.forbes.com/sites/andygreenberg/2012/01/30/hackers-demo-shows-how-easily-credit-cards-can-be-read-through-clothes-and-wallets/

20. Use the same "secret question" for casual online purchases that you use for your bank. That way when I hack the online site I get both your credit information and your "secret question" and answer.

21. Download phone apps from mistrusted sources. Allow it to access all of your data. It will let us install malware on your phone and see what you do.

22. Leave your smart phone unprotected against viruses and phishing schemes. It's not that smart, and it gives me access to everything that's on it and connected to it.

23. I love it when I learn about your pre-approved credit offers from your banks. That's like a scene in the stock market where I learn about juicy insider stock information — I violently rush to it so I'll be the first to get it. If you tell your banks to stop sending you any pre-approved credit card offers (Call 888-5-OPTOUT), how can I even get my hands on one of your credit cards?

24. If you get pre-approved credit cards or financial offers in your child's name, just ignore them. That way I'll have years to use their ID and create a false identity for them.

25. I love your predictable passwords. Who would guess that your password is your son's birthday? Who would know that your password is your father's middle name and your favorite color? Well, me, of course! So please, do make your passwords as predictable as possible.

26. I also love your incredibly convoluted passwords. So you combined letters, numbers, and symbols to make a password that even YOU can hardly remember. It's completely random, so an identity thief like me can never guess it, right? Well, when it's so convoluted that you need to write it down, I can find that scrap of paper.

27. I can piggyback on your unsecured Wi-Fi connection. I tell you, that's an open door. As soon as I can get in into your unsecured Wi-Fi connection, there are a thousand other things I can do to get as much information as I can from you.

28. Do you love to do the shortcut and let your browser keep your information for future use? If you answer yes, you are part of the great 80% of computer users who don't care much about what they kind of information they store voluntarily in their computers. I just run a little program and voila—I can easily hijack your contact info and passwords. Laptop users are an easier target; by stealing their device, I am able to access ALL the information they opted to keep in that device.

29. Got a broken laptop or hard drive? Do you bring your broken gadgets to the nearest repair center in town? Hey, I do too! I normally go to local computer repair centers and sometimes find disgruntled employees who are tempted to sell recovered data from people's broken laptops or hard drives. So please keep on coming back to that store where you don't really know or trust anyone… let me keep on mining that juicy information about you!

30. Broken mobile phone, USB sticks, hard drive, PDA's, laptops, etc. Throw them away without cleaning the data out. I'll do my thing in reviving and recovering them until I can extract every piece of data from them.

31. If I call you from your bank asking you to verify your personal information so I can tell you something important about your account, please do so! This is one of the best ways for me to get your information. If someone calls from the bank, call them back and check the number!

32. Use your debit card at the gas station or grocery store. I'm the one standing right behind you working on my phone and taking a picture of your card (and watching your pin) as you swipe it. My camera phone works great!

33. Your Facebook profile can tell so much about you. Have you opened your Facebook profile recently and checked what supposedly confidential information you have broadcasted to everybody?

Let me give you this checklist: email address, phone number, personal website, education history, work history, interests... Add all of them together and you'll have a clone in just a matter of minutes.

So please, make sure to keep your profile public — keeping it private will make it difficult for an identity thief like me.

34. Do you really know me? Why did you accept my friend invite in Facebook? Perhaps, it's my profile pic. Perhaps, it's my Timeline image. Perhaps, it's my name. It really doesn't matter. I'd really love to know you — all the information your real friends post on your wall, your contact information indicated in your Info, and those pictures… yes, those pictures of yours that I can easily grab to make a fake profile.

35. Let's organize a social networking group in Facebook. I love networking groups in social networks. It allows me to participate in discussions and solicit important personal information from different members. I don't really have to get sneaky or dig for information — everyone inadvertently volunteers it.

36. I can stir your temper or tickle your fancy at your favorite forum sites. Forum sites allow me to scoop data from forum members. I can either correspond directly through replied posts or I can challenge someone into a very delicate and critical discussion that would involve exchange of personal information. People can be so trusting.

37. Please leave your contact information in my blog. That's an easy way for me to obtain your email, address and even phone number.

38. I love to be your girl. Invite me for a chat. It's the oldest trick in the planet: get to know the person and scoop in all the information you need about the other person's identity. I'm not really a hot girl or a charming gentleman with a carefully sculpted body but I sure know how to pretend like one.

39. I frequent dating sites. It's one of my favorite arenas. There are more than a million lonely people who try to find romance, or even an easy lay, in dating sites. These people often volunteer just about anything about themselves to win the heart, or the body, of the one they pursue. That's why dating sites are my hunting ground. I can pose as the very person anyone would really love to meet.

40. If you got an email from your bank or from Amazon, open that quick; don't even check the sender's e-mail address. That e-mail will ask you for your username and password — please do give it, so I can access your bank accounts or purchase from Amazon. That's called "phishing" — it's me, an identity thief, giving you a website or e-mail that pretends to be something you can trust.

41. I have parasites working for me obtaining personal information from your computer.

And I can deploy them through e-mails posing as from legitimate sources, or I can simply transfer them to you during one of our chat or social network correspondences. So please do not put up a firewall or install an anti-virus on your computer, it hurts my chances of installing a spyware on your device!

42. I have a bogus job vacancy; you are certainly welcome to apply. Your cover letter and your resume summarize just everything about you. What's even better is I can use equip myself with all that information and become YOU.

43. I have an item for sale on Craigslist or Ebay. I can post an item that you might be interested in buying. It doesn't really matter if the item is real or not, or if I actually have the item, but as long as we correspond and you provide me payment details and all—everything just works perfectly fine for me. If you do use eBay, make sure you use the secure payment structure they provide!

44. Please answer my survey. It's just a survey anyway; it won't do you any harm. On the contrary, going through surveys that I send you through email or through my website or through Facebook allow me to embed "phishing" elements that can collect data from you — which you will voluntarily give, of course.

45. Knock, knock. I'm from the Bureau of Census. Sometimes, I do pose as a representative from the Bureau of Census or another government agency or non-profit institution and conduct interviews at the comfort of your home.

Often people just let me in, offer me a drink and then succumb to my flawless interviewing skills and charm.

46. I am your friendly neighborhood salesman. Posing as a representative of the national Bureau of Census is easy. Posing as a door-to-door salesman is easier. Same tactics, similar approach, exactly the same results.

47. I can be that sexy girl who sits beside you at the bar. Now that you've learned a few of the things you're not supposed to know about identity thieves and you're talking to a stranger, wouldn't you be more suspicious enough and be vigilant to police your surroundings?

Stealing Identities with Style

How Do Identity Thieves Do It?

A typical (and the often successful) identity thief normally looks and acts like any ordinary person. Not at all flamboyant, not at all James Bond-ish, not at all weird looking: they look like just a plain, ordinary, law-abiding citizen.

In short, an effective identity thief doesn't walk around carrying a big sign on his or her forehead reading: "I AM SUSPICIOUS LOOKING; I MIGHT BE AN IDENTITY THIEF!"

In fact, the best identity thieves are the ones who remain invisible. Why would you even suspect a person who is dumpster diving? How would you even trace where that fake e-mail from the IRS came from?

Identity thieves succeed because they themselves *do not disclose their identities.*

Identity Thieves Steal by Not Stealing

Dumpster diving, scanning information through public records, collecting someone else's trash, gathering garbage from banks or from insurance offices, and posing as a door-to-door salesman — these are things that old-school identity thieves do. Do you see something in common among these activities?

These activities do not necessarily qualify as stealing. If an identity thief gets your information from papers found in the trash, it is information *you voluntarily gave up.* Same as with answering a bogus survey or a fake questionnaire: YOU gave the thief your information; they did not force it away from you.

Even thieves who buy information from the black market (this could be an underground hacker's website or individuals or groups who sell stolen public information) do not steal forcibly — the reason why your information is readily available in the market anyway is because at one point in time, YOU gave away that information.

What Else Should You Know About Identity Theft?

- **Identity theft is always evolving.** The game is constantly evolving to adapt to the counter-measures being developed and enforced by authorities. Identity thieves are often two or three steps ahead of authorities that try to catch them.

- **There's no such thing as being "*too cautious*."** Banks already sell your information with only tacit consent. If you live in the wired world, getting access to any kind of data is as easy as getting a cigarette. Maybe easier.

- **Identity theft is addictive.** Being an identity thief for more than five years, one of my sources confirmed that the gig is really addictive. It pays for everything and it can get you anything you can buy.

- **Social networking sites are fertile playgrounds.** The advent of Facebook and Twitter and social networking sites makes a very good hunting ground for information. Pretending to be someone else in Facebook to attract interested parties is common.

- **A Credit or Debit card with an ID picture on it can be safe.** Well, "can" be safe is an overstatement. Nevertheless, most identity thieves will really not attempt to use a credit card with an ID picture because that's just a really dumb move. A workaround to that would be to just use the credit card for online purchases.

- **Identity thieves hate American Express.** Perhaps, it's one of the most hated credit cards because it always asks for the owner's (or the user's) Zip code. In most instances, identity thieves try to shy away from Amex as much as possible.

- **Your Smart Phone is a target.** While most people now secure their computers, many people have not realized the security holes in their smart phones. Stealing information from unsecured smart phones is a growing business.

Has Someone Stolen Your Identity?

How would you know if your identity has been stolen?

My research shows the statistics of identity theft in this country and around the world.

- Every 5 seconds there is a new victim of identity theft.
- Fraud amount per victim is on average $4,607.
- Out-of-pocket costs were $631 per incident (paying off fraudulent debt and legal and other fees).

- Average time spent by victims resolving the problem — 330 hours
- Medical Identity Theft affected over 1.5 million people last year a cost of 41.3 billion dollars. (Ponemon Institute)

Criminal cases arising from illegal exploitation of stolen identities have increased steadily.

The victims don't get any remuneration for the damages done to their reputations, their credit and their legal or medical records. All these expenses are out of pocket, and easy to avoid if you take some simple precautions.

In order to avoid becoming part of the alarmingly depressing numbers of identity theft cases, first thing you got to do is to find out if your identity has been stolen. Here are three steps that can help you do that.

First Step: Know the Signs

Staying alert for suspicious activities and transactions in your accounts is critically important.

Always keep in mind that you can never be too cautious with your information.

The possible signs that your identity might be in jeopardy would be:

- **Inaccurate information in your credit report and bank statements.** Be on the lookout for fraudulent data on the reports and papers you get from your bank or merchant. Always validate how your pertinent personal information such as name, address(es), Social Security number, phone numbers, and birth dates are indicated in the forms.

- **Unexplainable transactions in your accounts.** If you can't remember having made a certain transaction, always make a phone call to your bank or merchant and verify.

- **Undelivered mail or bills.** Call your bank or creditor for follow-up. Undelivered mail or bills can mean that the thief has stolen them from your doorstep or mailbox. Or they can have stolen your account and updated the billing and ship-to address to their designated location.

- **Credit cards that you didn't apply for suddenly arrive through mail.** These could possibly be just pre-approved credit cards offered by your merchants as part of their promo. However, it's always better to check with them and ask if there was an application or replacement request made that prompted them to send new cards. If these cards are in the name of one of your children, respond right away!

- **Loan or credit is denied.** Or you are offered credit with unsatisfactory credit terms and values. This might be because the thief has already amassed a ridiculous amount of debt in your account name.

- **You keep receiving calls or e-mails from your merchants about things you didn't buy.** When you encounter something like this, call your merchant and check in on it right away!

- **Checks, wallets and other sensitive finan-cial documents are nowhere to be found.** It could be that you just misplaced them or you left them somewhere. Either way, it's not safe to be complacent and disregard the possibility that you might have inadvertently left them somewhere public or they might have been stolen.

- **Your contacts have been receiving e-mails you didn't send.** If this happens, chances are your e-mail account has been compromised, and possibly, all other accounts tied to that e-mail address. Make sure you contact the concerned websites and ask for a change of password or disable the account.

- **Someone told you that they found an Internet profile matching yours.** The same personality, name, and even profile picture is on another person's Facebook, Twitter, or forum profile. This is a classic case of identity theft in the Internet Age. Report that person's profile to the administrator or customer service. After that, make sure to weed out your friends and contacts list, and make your profile private.

- **Unexplained medical bills.** Someone may be using your identity for medical benefits.

- **Lost access to your e-mail, Facebook, Twitter, etc.** Your account may have been compromised. Contact the administrator or customer service, and ask for a password reset.

Knowing the signs and understanding how identity thieves work can certainly reduce your likelihood to become a victim of identity theft.

Second Step: Monitor Your Personal Information

Keeping an eye on your personal information is critical in finding out if you have been a victim of identity theft. A routine monitoring of your personal information can make a huge difference — you can easily stop theft at its early stages, before things get worse.

Two of the basic pieces of personal information that allow you to detect suspicious activities would be your financial statements and credit reports. These pieces of information are immediately available and you can easily track them.

Financial Statements

Your financial statements such as account balances and billing reports will show you every detailed transaction and activities within a specific timeframe. If you keep records of these financial statements or if you request for a consolidated report, you will have a historical data that you can use for referencing your financial transactions.

Should any fraudulent transaction occur or if you find some suspicious entries in your financial statements, there's a possibility that the thieves have gained access to your bank accounts.

It's important to clarify the entries first with the merchant or bank in order to understand what those are and how they got into your statements before reporting anything to authorities. Do it quickly though, because if it is identity theft, the thief could be cleaning out your account right now.

Annual Credit Reports

Under amended federal laws regarding credit protection, you are entitled to receive a free annual credit report at your request. You can use to find fraudulent activity.

Free annual credit reports are available if you get in touch with national consumer reporting agencies through the following methods:

- Visit www.annualcreditreport.com

- Call the toll-free number 877-322-8228

- Fill out the Annual Credit Report Request form from the FTC website (www.ftc. gov/credit), and mail it to Annual Credit Report Service: PO Box 105281, Atlanta GA 30348-5281

You can also contact other consumer reporting companies, for a fee of around $9.50, to send your copies of your credit reports. Some of these reliable companies are:

- Equifax: www.equifax.com; Toll-free number at 800-685-1111

- TransUnion: www.transunion.com; Toll-free number at 800-916-8800

- Experian: www.experian.com; toll free number at 888-EXPERIAN (888-397-3742)

Credit Reports

Your credit report reveals a lot about you, more than you can imagine. It contains your account information, your bank account references, the bills that you're paying, and credit card numbers, to name a few.

Here are things that can guide you in investigating your credit reports:

- Check if your personal information is correct—name, addresses, credit cards.

Make sure you check all the addresses and names on the credit report and make sure that there are no extras or errors.

- Check for any new credit accounts that you never requested.

- Make sure all the correct information is only recorded once.

- Check for purchases and other debts that you didn't make.

- Check if your payment history has been reflected correctly.

- Check for your outstanding balances.

- Compare your current credit statements based on the historical data coming from your annual credit reports.

- Check your credit standing

- Pay particular attention to credit inquiries. See who is asking about your credit and if you gave them permission.

Whatever inaccuracies and inconsistencies you can find should be promptly reported and investigated further. Inaccurate personal information, such as an unfamiliar address should be checked out thoroughly as it could be someone else using your identity. Familiarize yourself with the procedures established by the Fair Credit Reporting Act to correct fraudulent information on your credit reports properly.

For any inconsistencies in your credit report, you must make sure you call your bank or merchant about the fraudulent activities. Clarify every entry that you find questionable and ask them to investigate further for a possible data breach.

If an identity thief has gained access to your credit information, you'll definitely find abnormal behavior in your credit reports. Your historical report and careful investigation should be able to detect these abnormal behaviors.

Third Step: Check Your Credit Score

Your credit score tells everything about your creditworthiness. Once an identity thief steals your credit information and start using it without paying the dues, your credit score will likely go down.

The negative effect of identity theft to your credit score is immediately recognizable and embarrassing. This results to your lower credit upstanding and an unsatisfactory image to your creditors.

When the time comes when you badly need a loan, your chances of qualifying will seriously be compromised. Not only that, you will be pestered by the number of collectors chasing you for debts you didn't create.

So if you find that your credit score is on its way to a surprising nosedive then it's likely that you are now a victim of identity theft. The thief is already enjoying your credit card freely and you're the one who suffers.

Credit Monitoring Services

You can employ a credit monitoring service to keep an eye and scrutinize every detail in your accounts all the time. This comes with a fee; but it can be very convenient if you are too busy to watch over your accounts at a regular basis.

Credit monitoring service agencies can alert you immediately if they find any possible fraudulent transactions or entries. They can also provide or suggest an immediate action to correct the errors. These agencies provide a wide variety of services for credit monitoring and protection.

Subscribing to these credit monitoring service companies requires you to understand what they're offering. Diligent and careful research is recommended.

You can call a consumer protection agency, the State Attorney General, or a local Better Business Bureau to check if any complaints were filed against your prospective credit monitoring service agency.

Making Sure Your Child is Safe from Identity Thieves

Another interesting area in identity theft investigation is the rising number of child identity theft. Identity thieves who prey on a minor's social security information don't get detected for years until the child has reached legal status to apply for credit.

There hasn't been much action in the country in implementing safety protection for a child's personal information. Identity thieves can obtain the information directly from hospitals, schools, daycare centers, or sports leagues.

While data breaches from these sources are very common because of the lack of security, there are even cases of data breaches that occur upon the assignment of Social Security numbers to newly born babies.

The work of cyber-criminals who steal (or replicate for that matter) identities from new-born babies has become much more complex and immediate nowadays. The reason is that the nature of Social Security number assignment is predictable.

The first three digits of the Social Security number references the region where the number is issued and the last six numbers tied to the identity of the baby is using a predictable sequence.

Because of the predictability in the generation of new Social Security numbers for newborn babies, many identity thieves are able to crack down these numbers as soon as they're issued. Moreover, the information is sold to a black market for identity thieves.

The usual notion that a child's personal information is safe because no one is really interested with it is no longer true. The most important thing that you need to keep in mind is safeguarding your child's personal information before someone gets a hold of it.

In cases of suspected child identity theft, here are possible guidelines you can do to find out if your child's identity is stolen:

- When asking for your family's credit reports, an unusual report on your minor child is a RED FLAG. Your minor child is not supposed to be receiving credit reports because he or she is not yet entitled to apply for credit.

- You can ask your local authorities to perform an in-depth investigation of your child's Social Security activities. This might include requests for credit applications, IDs, driver's license, loans, as well as public activities such as medical, legal, business and other transactions.

Presently, there hasn't been much focus on determining child identity theft until the minor reaches legal age. So, it's advisable that safety precautions and vigilance is employed in order to avoid criminals getting hold of your minor child's personal information.

Other Resources

FTC: Signs of Identity Theft:
http://www.consumer.ftc.gov/articles/0271-signs-identity-theft

FTC: Detecting Medical Identity Theft:
http://www.consumer.ftc.gov/articles/0171-medical-identity-theft#Detecting

Detecting Child Identity Theft: http://www.
identitytheftassistance.org/pageview.php?cate
id=94#KeepPersonalInformation

http://www.ftc.gov/bcp/edu/pubs/con-
sumer/idtheft/idt08.pdf

Detecting Criminal Identity Theft: http://
www.identitytheftassistance.org/pageview.
php?cateid=94#KeepPersonalInformation

What to Do If Your Identity has been Stolen

You won't have the luxury of being laid-back if you suspect that your identity has been stolen. What you need to keep in mind is to *act quickly to stop further damage*.

Identity thieves can wreak havoc and mayhem on your personal finances as well as your life. You can't dismiss what they can do as something that can be easily resolved. In fact, resolving an identity theft case can be extremely difficult.

The very best thing that you can do is take back control of your identity and personal finances. In cases like this you might be at a loss—almost no one expects to be a victim of identity theft. But you don't have to worry. I have put together the following information and resources to make it as straightforward as possible.

Make Sure Your Identity Has Been Stolen

If you notice charges on your credit cards or in your bank accounts that you do not recognize, start by calling the bank right away and asking them about the charges. I've had this happen several times, and it's often a bank error. But take this as a sign and get your credit report and check it out.

If you notice errors on your credit report, call the reporting agency. While it's been getting better, the credit reporting agencies do have a history of creating errors in credit reports that have nothing to do with identity theft.

If you notice errors or extra charges in your medical bills, call your medical company or insurance agency.

In my personal experience, often these are actually clerical errors. BUT, do make sure that they are clerical errors, and if you see errors across several accounts take more drastic action. Also, any of these things is an excellent reason to take 15 minutes, get your credit reports, and look them over!

In any case, if you are at all suspicious, then place a fraud report!

Place a fraud alert.

Call one of the credit reporting companies and ask for an initial fraud alert on your credit report. It's free and it makes any business that is going to open an account in your name actually check your identity before issuing credit. It lasts for 90 days and is a great stop-gap measure to prevent further damage from happening, or to take the time to explore whether your accounts have actually been stolen, or some other error has occurred.

Get your free credit reports and review them.

Contact all three credit companies and get your free reports. If there are errors, this will allow you to start to put together a file with the extent of the damages.

At this point it's great to get organized as many of the forms you'll have to fill out have the same information in them. Create a paper file or online folder to keep all the information you collect in.

Once you've gotten your free reports, write down every account that has errors. I suggest that you put it into a spreadsheet.

First contact the credit reporting agency to make sure that the errors are not clerical.

Talk with someone in the fraud department. Make sure you write down who you talk to and when you talked to them. Follow up in writing using certified mail so you have a record of the communication.

Write Down All Suspicious Activities

If you suspect that the errors are not clerical, then start to pull together your documents. Prepare a list of fraudulent activities that you can reference or present later on to the authorities or the duped organizations concerned.

The following is helpful information that you may need during filing a report:

- Fraudulent changes in your personal information

- Fraudulent activities and transactions using your personal information

- Suspicious entries in your financial statements and credit reports

- Complete details of fraudulent entries in your billing statements such as date of transaction, items purchased, the merchandise or services that were purchased, the amount credited, etc.

- Complete details of the fraudulent entries in your bank account such as actual amount lost, the transaction date, the place of transaction (if indicated), etc

- Moreover, it's important to take note of the following scenarios in order for authorities to trace how the identity thief started collecting your personal information:

- When you noticed your mail stopped arriving.

- When you noticed some personal effects containing your personal information were missing. These effects include credit cards, checks, insurance policies, medical bills, loan applications, etc.

- When you lost access to your email, social network sites login, online banking login, etc.

- When you noticed suspicious behaviors in your browser or computer.

- If you lost your wallet, it's important to take note of the day you first noticed it was missing.

- When you noticed obvious physical breaches of your mailbox, lockers, etc.

- Details of your online transactions such as job applications, forum group registration, online shopping, online chat, dating site access, etc.

- If someone was following you or acting suspiciously, any details you can remember about them are helpful.

Every single detail of events and activities are important in filing your report to the appropriate authorities. A complete detailed list of these events and activities provides the information needed for tracking the beginning of the crime, the breadth of the damage, the primary suspects, and the current status of the whole crime.

You need to ensure all your data is validated and supported with necessary documents and evidence. These things will also be used as preliminary evidence for possible judicial proceedings in the future when the identity thief is caught.

Contact the businesses with errors

Make a list of every company that has errors. If they are new accounts, make sure you notate the time they were opened and the balance information. If it is usage of your current accounts, go through your account statements and write down every suspicious activity and contact the bank and the merchant.

Again, contact the fraud department. Write down the time and date of your call, who you talked with and the outcome and next steps (this works great in a spreadsheet). Now follow each of those conversations up with a mailed letter return receipt so you can have a record of the correspondence.

Close All Suspected Accounts and Freeze Credit

To stop further damage to your bank accounts and credit status, you may choose to close all affected accounts down.

Illegal credit spending as well as unauthorized new credit requests and applications should immediately be stopped.

1. Call your credit card company and report your card as stolen. Ask them to cut off your card instead of blocking the lost card and issuing you a replacement. You don't want the new card to go to the thief!

2. Call your bank and ask them to freeze all transactions: both withdrawal and deposits. Freezing your account will stop access to the identity thief who gained access to your bank records.

3. Report your concern to the three national consumer reporting companies:

   • Experian at 1-888-EXPERIAN (397-3742). Check out their website: www.experian.com. Alternatively, you can send mail to PO Box 9554, Allen, TX 75013

   • Equifax at 1-888-525-6285. Check out their website: www.equifax.com. You can also send mail to PO Box 740241, Atlanta, GA 30374-0241

   • TransUnion at 1-800-680-7289. Check out their website: www.transunion.

com. You can also send mail to the
Fraud Victim Assistance Division, PO
Box 6790, Fullerton, CA 92834-6790

If you immediately cut off the sources of funds,
a financial identity thief will stop using your
information. If they have assumed your identity
completely, this can also be used to help track
them down.

What Does Credit Freeze Mean?

A credit freeze restricts creditors and other third
party merchants' access to your credit report, until
such a time that the credit freeze is lifted. Most
merchants and credit companies check your credit
report before issuing new credit. If a credit freeze
is in effect then no one can access your credit until
it is un-frozen. This stops anyone from being able
to get credit in your name (even you). If you need
credit, you can temporarily un-freeze your credit
so that the merchant can access it for a limited
time. This stops the identity thief from opening
new accounts under your name.

The good thing about credit freeze is that it will not affect your credit score. In addition, it won't keep you from getting a free annual credit report nor restrict you from buying one.

The laws on credit freeze vary from state to state. Some states provide free credit freeze options. Other states allow only identity theft victims to apply for a credit freeze while other states allow just about anyone. There may be fees upon temporary lifting of a credit freeze or formal removal of it.

Many people actually use a credit freeze to deter identity theft. Here's an interesting article on the subject: http://usatoday30.usatoday.com/money/perfi/columnist/block/2007-10-08-credit-freeze_N.htm

Recovering from Your Identity Theft Problems

Now that you've taken the steps to resolve your identity theft case, and pretty much gathered all the documents you need for further actions in the future, it's now time to regain control of your identity.

Your bank accounts and credit score may be a mess; worse still, your identity may be more heavily compromised than you think. Recovering from these losses need urgency as much as possible to get you back what you have lost.

Create an Identity Theft Report

If someone has created a lot of debt in your name, the Fraud Report will help you handle debt collectors and businesses that are owed money from the person who stole your identity.

The report will help you:

- Get fraudulent information off your credit report

- Stop companies and debt collections agencies from harassing you to collect debt created by the identity thief, or from selling that debt to another company

- Place an extended fraud alert on your account

A fraud report consists of an FTC affidavit and a police report.

File a Complaint with the FTC

The Federal Trade Commission (FTC) has established a set of guidelines about complaint filing that you should follow if your personal information gets compromised.

The FTC advises people with stolen identity cases to immediately place fraud alerts. They further advise the victims to call the three national consumer reporting companies, and then contact the FBI for added in-depth investigation assistance.

The FTC enumerates two types of fraud alerts:

1. An initial alert, which is appropriate for cases of lost or stolen wallet as well as "phishing" scam victims. The initial alert entitles you to a free credit report from

the three nationwide consumer reporting companies. The initial alert stays on your credit report for no less than 90 days.

2. An extended alert, which is appropriate for identity theft cases where an "identity theft report" has been submitted to the three consumer reporting companies. Filing an extended alert entitles you to two free credit reports within the year. Your name will also be removed from marketing lists that are pre-screened for credit offers. The extended alert normally lasts up to 7 years.

Proof of identity is required when filing any of the two fraud alerts. Proof of identity includes, but is not limited to: Social Security number, legal name, address, phone number, and other personal information normally requested for credit purposes.

Businesses and establishments who see the fraud alert in your credit report will have to verify your identity before they can proceed in issuing you credit. They will have to contact you directly as part of their verification process. The inconvenient part in this process is that it will cause delays in obtaining a loan or credit.

But since your main purpose for filing for a fraud alert is to temporarily freeze your accounts and credit ability, the whole verification process should work to your advantage.

Before you submit a report to the Federal Trade Commission (FTC), you must remember the very first step we have, which is to gather all the pieces of evidence necessary to back up your complaint.

You will have to share important information to the FTC in order for them to work effectively with you. They will be able to also assist you in endorsing your case to law enforcement officials across the nations who will be able to investigate on your case, track down the thief and catch them.

Further, the FTC can also refer you to the appropriate government agencies as well as companies who provide further solutions to your problem.

You can fill out an online form for the complaint through the FTC website using the steps below. You can reach the Federal Trade Commission by phone at 1-877-IDTHEFT (438-4338); TTY: 1-866-653-4261. You can also send your mail to:

Identity Theft Clearinghouse
Federal Trade Commission
600 Pennsylvania Avenue, NW
Washington, DC 20580

How to submit a complaint to the FTC

1. Go to: https://www.ftccomplaintassistant.gov/
2. Submit a complaint
3. Save the complaint reference number
4. Print your FTC Identity Theft Affidavit
5. Print out this document as well as it will assist with your police report: http://www.consumer.ftc.gov/sites/default/files/articles/pdf/pdf-0088-ftc-memo-law-enforcement.pdf

You can also call the FTC at 877-438-4338

Report to the Police or Designated Investigation Officials

Your local police, the FBI, and other law enforcement agencies will only be able to assist you properly if you have enough evidence and paper trails for them to track the suspect and make a catch.

However, their role would just be secondary to your needs. These agencies won't be responsible in cutting off your connection with the identity thief. They are reinforcements in your battle to find out who stole your identity and took advantage of your personal information.

Nevertheless, the function of these agencies is critical in ensuring that you don't get victimized again. On top of that, they will be pivotal in the possibility of you being compensated for your damages and losses should the thief be caught in the future.

What If the Local Police Deny Your Request to File a Police Report?

There will be times when your local police will hesitate to file your complaint. In cases like this, you can ask them to file the complaint as a "<u>Miscellaneous Incident</u>" report. If nothing works, you can try another jurisdiction.

In addition, you can approach your state's Attorney General to determine if the state laws require the police to accept reports regarding identity theft.

For a list of every state's Attorney General, you can check out <u>www.naag.org</u> or you can try the Blue Pages of your phone directory or look online.

Filing Your Police Report

Always bring a printed <u>copy of the FTC ID Theft Complaint Form</u> together with your <u>cover letter</u> as well as <u>supporting documents</u>. Your cover letter should explain why there's a need for you to file a police report. The ID Theft Complaint is also very important to identity theft victims.

Never forget to ask a copy of the Identity Theft Police Report. You can use this for disputes on fraudulent accounts, transactions, as well as debts that you will file to banks and credit card merchants in the future. In cases where your local police are not authorized to release such documents, make sure to have them sign your FTC ID Theft Complaint Form or let them write the police report number.

Resolving Issues with Your Bank and Creditors

It's important to work with your bank or credit card companies to resolve whatever issues have arisen. You need to personally deal with the respective banks and credit card companies until you reach an agreement on how to fix the problem.

Be sure to provide all the documents that will dispute every suspicious transaction that appeared on your bank and credit records. Provide a copy of your FTC ID Theft Complaint form so they can speed-up the resolution.

As soon as you have fixed issues with your bank or credit card companies, it's important to employ added security measures to prevent the same thing from happening again.

Resolving Criminal Violations Committed Under your Name

There are certain procedures that you have to undergo when your identity has been used for criminal activities. Though these procedures may vary from state to state, it's advisable to immediately seek help with your counsel or your local authorities in order to prevent wrong arrests, incorrect detentions, or unnecessary criminal proceedings.

Alert the authorities immediately so they can enforce standard operating procedures in containing the case. The local police, the FBI, or other government agencies will then conduct further investigations until your name is completely cleared.

Always have constant communication with the authorities in order to follow-up your case and speed-up the resolution. Otherwise, you will have limited opportunities for job applications, schools, and credit applications, among others if your name is not yet cleared.

To clear your name in court records, you will need to determine what state law will be able to help you with this. Contact the District Attorney's office to arrange procedures in clearing your name. You will also need to hire a defense attorney to represent you for potential court proceedings.

Lastly, you will have to contact your state's Department of Motor Vehicles (DMV) to investigate if the identity thief has been using your driver's license. You must advise them to flag your files for a possible fraud.

In addition, if the DMV can terminate your old driver's license and replace it with another, you should take that option. This still varies from state to state though. But it is essential to inquire about these services in order for you to regain control of your driver's license and freedom.

Other Resources

FTC: Recovering from Identity Theft: http://www.consumer.ftc.gov/features/feature-0014-identity-theft

https://www.privacyrights.org/fs/fs17a.htm

FTC: Recovering from Medical Identity Theft: http://www.consumer.ftc.gov/articles/0171-medical-identity-theft#Correcting

Detailed guidelines on recovering from medical identity theft: http://www.worldprivacy-forum.org/FAQ_medicalrecordprivacy.html

Recovering from Child Identity Theft: http://
www.idtheftcenter.org/artman2/publish/v_
fact_sheets/Fact_Sheet_120.shtml

Recovering from Criminal Identity Theft:
http://www.fbi.gov/about-us/investigate/
cyber/identity_theft

https://www.privacyrights.org/fs/fs17g-
CrimIdTheft.htm

Preventing Your Identity from Being Stolen

Most identity theft cases are a result of a lax of protection on someone's personal information. I admit to being guilty to that. But after my personal experiences of identity theft, I learned that I was extremely vulnerable, especially with my smartphone.

I was an easy target to identity thieves. I wasn't a vigilant type of person; and being fairly well known there was a lot of information about me in the public arena.

I've learned to be more careful now that I understand the pitfalls and pain of having my identity stolen.

I've learned how vulnerable we are, and that it's extremely important to safeguard your personal information while you can—while you are not yet a victim of identity theft. It's too late once you've learned you are a victim of identity theft.

Consider the stress of having to go through all those steps in trying to recover your lost identity plus the damages that you will never be repaid for. All those things are a nightmare.

I hate the idea of having my identity stolen from me (again). That's why I have formulated these guidelines that can help me (and you) prevent identity theft.

Some of the things that I highlight are everyday things that you may often overlook. While you don't intentionally overlook these things, unfortunately, not being vigilant enough in safeguarding your personal information makes you a lot more vulnerable to suspicious behavior and activities that happen in your surroundings.

Remember this: <u>preventing identity theft is far better than solving problems caused by it.</u>

Why You Should Protect Your Identity

Protecting your personal information is your responsibility. As such, it is a very simple responsibility but it entails very high consequences when neglected.

Nowadays, when the world runs with the infinite exchange of information, a wrong move in safeguarding your personal data could lead to identity theft. The results can be very difficult to fix and sometimes irreparable.

The exploitation can cause several damages on your finances, your credibility, as well as your innocence — you might have a criminal status even if you had not ever committed a crime.

If an identity thief uses your stolen identity for criminal reasons such as murder or terrorism, you'll most likely get invited for federal investigation (not the kind of invitation you can turn down!). Even if the case is resolved, you will be left with a dirty record associated with your name. With that record associated to your identity, it could be hard for you to apply for new jobs, or go to school, get a loan, or even get through an airport. In short, you would find it hard to live a normal life.

One solution for this would be an identity makeover, which normally comes in a form of a name change or a newly issued social security number. Once that's completed, the next thing that you will have to worry about is the trauma.

Trauma resulting from a case of identity theft might affect you in your everyday life for years. As a former victim of identity theft, you might develop a sense of paranoia in your future transactions.

Research indicates that someone victimized by an identity thief, especially if it's friends or family, can lose their basic ability to trust anyone, including family and friends.

There is also what they call *social trauma* where the community around the victim is the one traumatized by the victim's alleged exploits as a criminal or terrorist. The biggest problem underlying in here is that society can't be dictated.

Once a criminal record is associated to you, it would be very difficult for the public to remember that you didn't do it. Though it might enlighten people that your identity was stolen, the room for doubt and prejudice will always be there.

Social trauma then is very difficult to resolve and may take years to fade away.

Thus, the importance of protecting your personal information is critical.

Ten Basic Steps to Protect Your Personal Information

The basics of personal information protection are not at all very difficult or costly. Simply keeping your personal effects in a safe and locked place will sometimes be enough.

However, there are things that you cannot just put in a safe. Your transaction behavior, for example, is a gold mine for identity thieves. In order to keep yourself protected, here are ten pretty basic things that you can do to safeguard your personal information.

1. **In all cases, protect your Social Security number.** Never carry your card with you in your wallet nor leave it in any accessible drawer. Make sure to keep it in a very secure location. I suggest that you memorize your Social Security number so you won't have to take your card with you every time you need to use or write down your Social Security number.

2. **Make sure sensitive items are kept in a secure place.** Items such as credit card and bank statements, checkbooks, powers of attorney, and health insurance policies should be locked away in a safe or a sturdy drawer.

3. **Use the shredder.** Don't just throw anything out on the trash; make sure to shred your documents. Don't exempt anything. If it fits into the shredders mouth, let the

shredder eat it. Remember: <u>the identity thief can use whatever you throw out in the trash</u>.

4. **Go paperless**. You might not be a fan of receiving electronic statements or bills, but nowadays it might be the safer way to transact. However, you would need to ensure that your computer is adequately protected against spyware so no cyber-criminal can get access to your logins. If you want to receive your letters the traditional way, get a secured and locked mailbox.

5. **Call 888-5OPTOUT** to stop creditors from sending you pre-approved credit offers.

6. **In the event of a stolen or lost wallet**, make sure to contact all banks as well as credit card companies immediately to report the loss. File the necessary police reports and ensure that your other personal information is covered. This not only applies to your wallet, but also any personal effects that might contain very

sensitive information about you as a
whole.

7. **Be more vigilant of your surroundings**.
    Identity thieves are everywhere; they can
    be the unassuming and friendly waiter
    who accommodates all your orders with a
    smile, or the stranger who offers you assis-
    tance as you move your way to the ATM.
    For your protection, always make sure to
    safeguard your personal information and
    keep it far away from any person's access.

8. **Stay away from strange ATMs**. If you
    notice something strange-looking on
    the ATM, it would be better to just find
    another one. Don't run the risk of falling
    into an identity thief's traps. ATMs that
    have strange-looking devices on the ATM
    card slots could be rigged with mecha-
    nisms that can skim off data from your
    card's magnetic strip.

9. **Monitor your bank and credit accounts**.
    Don't only do this whenever you have
    a stolen identity case. It's more than

recommended to monitor your bank and credit accounts and be vigilant. This will help you in the long run as you will be able to scrutinize every detail of your credit report that you don't understand.

10. **Review your credit reports at least once a year.** You can get free access to all three of your credit reports one time a year. Take 15 minutes and look through them to make sure they are free from error. If there are errors, get them fixed before you need credit!

In the instance that you find anomalies in your credit reports and financial statements, you now know what agency to call to report the anomalies. This practice will teach you not to brush off any suspicious entry in your records. Always keep in mind that all entries in your records are important.

Cyber Protection 101

Since most identity thieves now work with technology, it's also equally important to understand the fundamental methods of cyber protection.

Identity thieves are more adept with technology than regular citizens. They prey on people who have little or no knowledge in computers and the cyber world. The Internet proves to be an open highway for thieves to access information and wreak havoc.

On top of that, identity thieves also work with cyber criminals who perform their crimes online. These cyber criminals have all the technology to do just about anything that is requested from them by their customers. They even have subterranean black market sites that provide everything a hacker or an identity thief needs.

If the identity thief needs some personal information, he or she can just go to the black market site and shop for readily available personal information. Or they can hire someone who can penetrate highly secured data sources just to extract the information that they need.

However, these things, though they seem to be highly impossible to counteract, can be prevented. The main tools that these people use are holes in the system. As soon as they can find a hole in your computer's system, it's easier for them get in and get what they need.

Even deadlier than a lack of an anti-virus program are behavioral holes that most ordinary users commit such as opening spam emails, visiting suspicious websites, downloading unverified materials, frequenting torrent sites, and entertaining posers in social networking sites such as Facebook, MySpace, Tumbler, and Twitter.

Thus, equipping yourself with the basic set of behaviors for protecting your personal information in the cyber world is required. This basic set of behaviors should be common practice when using your computer, tablet or smart phone, even for the simplest of activities.

- Install the necessary security software for your computer and smart phone to prevent virus, spyware, and other malware attacks.

- Install a firewall so no data-collecting bots can penetrate your technology.

- Turn on pop-up blockers and other necessary protection for your Internet browser.

- Don't allow your browser to store recently used information for future use.

- Clear the cache, cookies and history of your browser weekly. Or if you want to go hardcore in cyber security, do it every day.

- Stop opening spam emails or suspicious emails that pretend that they are coming from legitimate sources.

- Don't click on links if you are not sure where it will go.

- Add extra protection to your e-mail login as well as your online banking login by using more complicated and random passwords.

- When prompted to supply a security question, make sure to provide something that's not obvious. Choose security questions even your best friends won't know the answer to!

• Never entertain Facebook friend requests or Twitter follows from people you don't know.

• When someone invites you for a chat, hesitate and try as much as possible to investigate whom that person might be (or use a 'pen name' yourself).

• Don't click any shared Facebook links.

• Adjust the privacy settings on your Facebook for added security. Make sure your profile is not set to public.

• Don't use games or applications in Facebook that ask for your personal information, unless the developers are trusted.

• Be careful accessing dating sites. These are the hunting ground of cyber-criminals. Moreover, dating sites are home to a lot of posers who will trick you in accessing their profile and exchanging information with them.

- Stop accessing porn sites.

- Never enter your personal information when being asked to if you want to comment on a blog post, unless the blog system has a good reputation for privacy such as WordPress or Blogger.

- When using the contact page of a website with which you don't trust, make extra precautions and avoid supplying very sensitive personal information.

- Use your anti-virus software to scan attached files or documents you receive through e-mails, chat, video conferencing, and other mediums of delivery.

- Run a scan on your computer regularly to ensure it's free of any malware.

- Turn off your computer after use.

- Set a password to your computer so no one can use it without your permission. If you want other people to use it without the need to supply a password, make sure to create a Guest account.

- When making a purchase online, make sure to use the most verified and secured way to check out your items. More importantly, don't allow the site to store your information for future use. Always clear the cache and cookies after your purchase.

- Exercise extreme caution when transacting in low-security online shopping sites.

- If you are applying for a job, verify first if the poster is legitimate before sending in your resume that contains a lot of your personal information.

- Don't just click whatever "free offers" or "discounts" you can see on shopping sites.

Creating the Best and the Strongest Password

Even without opening yourself up to obvious avenues of cyber identity theft, your web accounts can still be compromised if you have a weak password.

Weak passwords are those that are derived from your personal information (e.g., a combination of birthdays, lyrics to your favorite song, your dog's name), or are made up of something common (e.g. a single random word found in the dictionary, a famous phrase from a commercial).

The reason why these passwords are weak is because they are easily predictable.

Once you become a target of identity thieves, they will probably be able to deduce a password made up of things that are of personal importance to you.

Passwords made of a common phrase or a single word are also easy because they can be guessed by a software that brute-forces its way by inputting common phrases and all the possible words in a dictionary.

A strong password, therefore, is: 1) Something that cannot be deduced from your personal life; and 2) Something that cannot be brute-forced by a computer program.

Contrary to popular belief, mixing random lowercase and uppercase letters, numbers, and symbols does not necessarily make a strong password. In many cases, software that is used to brute-force its way into cracking passwords can easily guess a short password consisting of random letters, numbers, and symbols.

To make this random password secure, you need to make it long so it couldn't be possibly brute-forced by a software. The problem is, a long password consisting of random letters and characters will certainly be a monster to remember. You would probably need to hack your own account because you will forget what your password is. And of course, writing it down on a piece of paper or storing it in your mobile phone will make you more vulnerable than secure.

An ideal password will have the following characteristics:

1. Be at least 8 characters long.
2. Have a combination of lower case and UPPER CASE letters
3. Have at least one number and one symbol

Below are some resources for helping you to create a strong password that you can remember!

http://www.makeuseof.com/tag/create-strong-password-forget/

http://windows.microsoft.com/en-US/windows-vista/Tips-for-creating-a-strong-password

The Case Against Identity Theft Protection Services

At this point you might be thinking that an Identity Theft Protection Service is a great way to save yourself from the hassle of having to take measures to protect your own identity. That's what I thought until I found this interesting article by Consumer Reports.

http://www.consumerreports.org/cro/2012/02/debunking-the-hype-over-id-theft/index.htm

Basically, it states that most fraud is someone getting a hold of your existing account information, and there are simple free alerts you can request from your financial institution that will let you know when a purchase over a certain amount (say $100) is made on your account, or if your balances are low. For debit and credit cards, if you find out about the situation in the first few days, there is much less liability. If, on the other hand, you never check your balances and don't balance your checkbook or credit accounts, so it takes longer for you to find out about it, you could have more liability.

If you are concerned about someone opening new accounts in your name, get a credit freeze (discussed earlier). This makes it so that no one can access your credit information without the freeze being removed. It might make it a little more tedious to get credit yourself, but it stops a thief in their tracks!

The challenge with Identity Theft Protection Services is that they don't always catch it if your identity is stolen, but having them can make you complacent and less likely to take responsibility for keeping track of your own records.

Conclusion

PROTECT YOURSELF FROM IDENTITY THIEVES. Simple precautionary measures such as being more vigilant to your surroundings are always a best practice.

You really can't tell whom you'll bump into in the future but whatever the case may be, you are already prepared.

So look through this book again, and decide one thing that you are going to do today to make yourself more secure.

Will you?

- Add a password to your smart phone?

- Change some of your lame passwords to better ones?

- Get your free credit reports and see if there is any weird information on them?

Just take one step toward having a safer life!